GROUNDBREAKERS

ALPHARETTA

Louis Pasteur

Ann Fullick

Heinemann Library
Chicago, Illinois

Designed by AMR
Illustrated by Art Construction
Originated by Ambassador Litho
Printed in Hong Kong/China

05 04 03 02 01
10 9 8 7 6 5 4 3 2 1

Library of Congress Cataloging-in-Publication Data
Fullick, Ann, 1956-
    Louis Pasteur / Ann Fullick
        p. cm. -- (Groundbreakers)
    Includes bibliographical references and index.
    ISBN 1-57572-373-5 (library)
    1. Pasteur, Louis, 1822-1895--Juvenile literature. 2.
Scientists--France--Biography--Juvenile literature. 3.
Microbiologists--France--Biography--Juvenile literature. [1. Pasteur, Louis, 1822-1895.
2. Scientists. 3. Microbiologists.] I. Title. II. Series.

Q143.P2 F85 2000
579'.092--dc21
[B]   00-035015

Acknowledgments
The Publishers would like to thank the following for permission to reproduce photographs:
Bridgeman Art Library, p. 4; Corbis, pp. 5, 27; Institut Pasteur Musée, pp. 6, 7, 9, 14, 15, 24, 25,
32, 33, 35, 36; Mary Evans Picture Library, pp. 8, 19, 30, 34, 37; AKG photo, pp. 10, 26; Hulton
Getty, p. 11; Science Photo Library, pp. 12, 16, 20, 31, 40, 41; J. Allan Cash, pp. 17, 28; Oxford
Scientific Film, p. 18; Trip/H. Rogers, p. 38; Still Pictures, p. 39; Wellcome Library, p. 42;
Collections/Sandra Lousada, p. 43.

Cover photograph reproduced with permission of Science Photo Library.

Every effort has been made to contact copyright holders of any material reproduced in this
book. Any omissions will be rectified in subsequent printings if notice is given to the Publisher.

Some words are shown in bold, **like this.** You can find out what
they mean by looking in the glossary.

Contents

Turbulent Times

France in the early nineteenth century was a country in turmoil. The Napoleonic wars were over, and people's lives were getting back to normal, but the legacy of the **French Revolution**—when so many great thinkers and scientists had been sent to their deaths at the **guillotine**—still hung over the country. On December 27, 1822, Louis Pasteur was born into these turbulent times.

A hard life

In those days, most jobs were done by hand, and most people lived lives of constant physical labor. There was also little or no defense against disease. Children died young, women died from infection after childbirth, and men died from infected work injuries.

Because no one understood the causes of these diseases, no one could cure them. Louis Pasteur carried out an amazing amount of scientific work during his lifetime, but perhaps most important was his work on **infectious diseases.** By the end of his life, he had explained how infectious diseases were spread and made **vaccination** against some of them possible.

In the early nineteenth century, life was hard for everyone, but it was hardest of all for the poor. These Breton farmers in northern France are digging up potatoes.

A day to remember

In October 1831, when Louis was just eight years old, a rabid wolf made its way down from the mountains and went berserk, attacking people at random. Eight of the victims later developed rabies and died. Several people in Louis' village were bitten, and they all went to the blacksmith for the only known treatment for rabies—to have the wounds cauterized, or branded with red-hot iron. The young Louis Pasteur heard their dreadful screams, saw their terror, and smelled the burning flesh. In years to come, these images remained with him and drove him on with his research.

A great legacy

The legacy of Louis Pasteur is truly a great one. His lasting achievements include exciting new discoveries in chemistry; developing methods of preserving wine and milk; saving the silkworm industry; and producing explanations and cures for infectious diseases, including rabies.

The Pasteur Family

Louis drew this portrait of his mother, Jeanne, when he was a teenager. The drawings he did as a schoolboy were of an amazingly high standard, but none of his other schoolwork was as good.

The Pasteur family

The Pasteur family came from humble origins. For centuries, they had worked in the fields as agricultural workers and then as **tenant farmers.** Gradually, they had moved to become tradesmen, and Louis Pasteur's father, grandfather, and great-grandfather were all **leather tanners.**

Monsieur and Madame Pasteur

Louis's father, Jean-Joseph Pasteur, was drafted into the French army when he was twenty, and served with such distinction that he was awarded several medals. Jean-Joseph was proud to be part of a victorious French army under Napoleon and regarded these as his "glory days" for the rest of his life.

When Jean-Joseph returned to civilian life and his old trade of tanning in Salins, near the Swiss border, life must have seemed very dull compared to his adventures at war. However, before long he began courting a local gardener's daughter, Jeanne Etiennette Roqui, and in 1816, they were married. They soon moved to the nearby town of Dôle, and it was there that they started their family before moving to Marnoz and then to Arbois.

Brothers and sisters

Their first child was a son, but the joy following his birth soon turned to sadness when he died in infancy. Jeanne's second baby, born in 1818, was a daughter; four years later, Jean-Joseph and Jeanne welcomed another child—a boy—into the world. He was born on December 27, 1822, and they named him Louis—Louis Pasteur, a name that would become famous the world over. In the next few years, the family was completed with the birth of two more daughters, so Louis grew up in Arbois as the only boy among a family of girls.

Growing up

Louis seems to have had a fairly happy childhood, brought up to be loyal to the family, to work hard, and to take good care of money. His father hoped that he might one day become a teacher in the local school, leaving behind the messy, smelly world of tanning, and this seemed a possibility. Louis was a good, but not outstanding, student at the local school, a hard worker whose main talent seemed to be drawing!

By the time Louis drew this portrait of his father, a few years later, his other schoolwork had begun to improve. It was becoming obvious that he was destined to work with his brain and not just his hands.

Getting an Education

Louis did not excel during his early years in school, but as he got older, his intellect began to develop. He won many prizes at school and set his sights on the most prestigious colleges in Paris to continue his education and study to become a teacher.

The search for success

Louis decided to try for a place at the École Normale and went to study at a specialized boarding school in Paris. However, he was so homesick and unhappy that after a month he returned home to go back to his old school. The next year, he went on to a secondary school about 25 miles (40 kilometers) from home.

Four months before his eighteenth birthday, Louis earned his **baccalauréat.** His grades for every subject were "good" except for elementary science—these were "very good." This made Louis determined to study science, so he stayed on and worked for two more years to gain his baccalauréat in science. When he finally achieved this, his grade in physics was "passable," and in chemistry "mediocre," so his genius was still not evident!

Students who wanted to enter the École Normale had to work very hard to pass the difficult entrance exams. It was the best teacher training institute in France at that time, and Pasteur worked hard to get in.

Louis was finally offered a place at the École Normale, but his grades were among the lowest that year. Not satisfied, he turned down the offer and went back to the school he had previously left out of homesickness. This time he stayed, and gradually his hard work and determination began to be matched by his grades. When he finally tried again to enroll at the École Normale, he was ranked fourth on the list of candidates in the science section.

The scientist emerges

Between the years of 1843 and 1846, Louis Pasteur worked away at the École Normale. He studied hard, did a little bit of teaching, and took up a number of research projects. In 1847, he was made a doctor of science and quickly made his mark in the scientific world.

Louis blossomed during his time as a student, and by the age of 24, he was beginning to have ideas that would inspire his research for many years to come.

Pleasing his father with a teaching career in some small French town no longer appealed to Louis. He now set his sights on a high-flying scientific career among the greatest scientists in Paris. But in 1848, revolution rocked the city of Paris, and the plans of Louis Pasteur, like those of so many others, were thrown into turmoil.

Revolution

The French National Guard lines up at the palace of Versailles. In 1848, Louis joined the National Guard, a municipal **militia** with the job of maintaining civil order. He also gave all of his savings, a sum of 150 francs, to the republic.

The first **French Revolution,** which changed the entire history of the nation and affected all of Europe, had begun in 1789. At the beginning of this later French revolution, in February 1848, Louis Pasteur and many others simply tried to keep out of the way. However, when the Second Republic was declared in April, it became impossible to remain on the sidelines any longer, and Louis joined the National Guard.

A personal loss

Reports of the fighting and difficulties in Paris spread like wildfire to the provinces. Back in Arbois, Louis's family—particularly his mother—worried about him a great deal. Paris and their only son seemed a long way away. At the end of May 1848, Jeanne Pasteur was suddenly taken ill and died of what appeared to be a burst blood vessel in the brain. Louis was grief-stricken, and blamed himself for the anxiety he had caused, which he was sure had contributed to his mother's death.

Louis's father now had sole responsibility for Louis's three sisters, all unmarried and in their twenties. A bad fever had left the youngest with severe learning disabilities, and she needed special care. In spite of the fact that it meant leaving Paris and all of his research, Louis asked to be transferred to a small-town post relatively close to his remaining family.

Life moves on

Louis was appointed professor of physics in Dijon in September, but he did not sctually start the job until December—he had some crucial research to finish in Paris before he moved. In spite of his concerns immediately after his mother's death, Louis did not stay close to his family for long—ambition drove him on. He had been in Dijon only a few weeks when he successfully applied for, and won, the post of assistant professor of chemistry at the University of Strasbourg. He started this new job in January 1849.

A whirlwind romance

Arriving in Strasbourg toward the end of January 1849, Louis immediately met Marie Laurent, the daughter of the university **rector.** By February 10, he was writing a formal letter of proposal to her father, asking permission to marry his daughter!

Louis obviously made a good impression on all concerned, because on May 29, 1849, when he was 26 years old, he and Marie were married. During the early years of his marriage, he settled into a period of very productive work, which was to bring him wide-ranging recognition.

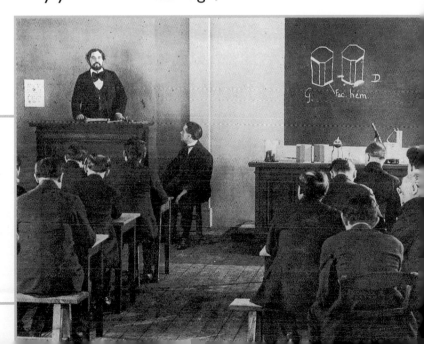

Louis Pasteur lectured at the University of Strasbourg. Although Louis threw himself into his teaching and research when he took up his post in Strasbourg, he also put a lot of effort into his personal life as he courted Marie Laurent.

Crystallography

When the young Louis Pasteur was searching for topics for the research for his doctorate at the École Normale in Paris, he became influenced by Auguste Laurent, a well-known scientist at the time. As a result, Pasteur began work on the **molecules** of water held within the **crystal** structures of various chemicals.

Solving the paratartrate riddle

Pasteur became skilled in the use of **polarized light** in the study of crystals. Normal light is made up of a mixture of light rays traveling in random directions, but in a beam of polarized light, the rays are all traveling in the same direction.

The German chemist Eilhardt Mitscherlich had found two chemicals that he thought were identical—**tartaric** acid and racemic acid (also known as paratartaric acid).

Crystals have different shapes and different numbers of faces, depending on which chemical they are made of. These copper sulfate crystals are sparkling as light reflects off their faces.

However, he was puzzled to find that while tartaric acid was **optically active,** meaning that it rotated polarized light to the right, paratartaric acid appeared to have no effect at all on polarized light. Pasteur's work solved this problem and provided a major breakthrough in the understanding of crystal structure.

By very careful observation of the paratartrate crystals, Pasteur found that some of the crystals had faces that bent polarized light to the right. Others had faces that bent light to the left. When mixed together in the normal compound, these canceled each other out and made it look as if the substance was optically inactive. Finally, he showed that a solution of right-hand crystals alone rotated polarized light to the right, while left-hand crystals alone rotated the light to the left. This meant that the effect on polarized light was due to differences in the molecules themselves—and it was these differences that affected the way the crystals formed.

Legend has it that in April 1848, when Pasteur made his discovery, he rushed out of his laboratory and hugged a chemistry lab assistant who happened to be walking down the hall! True or not, the story reflects Pasteur's excitement at his discovery.

There were personal excitements, too. In 1850, Louis and Marie celebrated the birth of their first child, a daughter named Jeanne, and in 1851, their only son, Jean-Baptiste, was born. Over the next few years, they added three more daughters to their family.

This is Louis Pasteur in 1857, at the age of 34, while dean of the Faculty of Sciences at Lille.

In September 1854, Louis Pasteur was officially appointed professor of chemistry and dean of the new **Faculty** of Sciences at the University of Lille in northern France. Part of the job of this new faculty was to use science to support and help the thriving local industries. Lille was then a center of mining and industrial activity in France. Pasteur took this aspect of his job description to heart, and it was a close association with local manufacturers that launched him on the next stage of his research career.

Pasteur the organizer

In his new position, Pasteur had to concentrate on the administration of the faculty as well as on his research. He quickly showed that this was another of his many talents, and soon introduced laboratory-based teaching for all the science subjects. Before this, science students had been given lectures and watched some demonstrations, but they had not worked in laboratories themselves. Learning science in this way must have been fairly dull and distant.

Pasteur also worked very hard at forging links between local industry and the faculty. He took students on trips to factories in Belgium, to look at the techniques they used to produce and purify metals. He also got them testing manures to be used in agriculture. He ran courses teaching the science behind some of the more important local industries—bleaching, sugar-making, and refining, and especially the **fermentation** and refining of the local specialty, beet **alcohol.**

Beets and Monsieur Bigo

One of the big businesses in the area around Lille was the fermentation of beet sugar to produce alcohol. Louis Pasteur became increasingly interested in the process of fermentation, although the reasons for this interest have never been entirely clear.

The story goes that one of Pasteur's students was the son of a local beet alcohol producer, Monsieur Bigo. When Bigo and others suffered a really difficult year, with fermentations that went wrong and produced little or no alcohol, he asked the illustrious teacher for advice. Pasteur made frequent visits to the factory and finally demonstrated that successful fermentation showed rounded yeast globules under a microscope, but if the fermentation went wrong, then long rod shapes were seen instead. He taught the workers to tell the difference, and to destroy batches that showed signs of rods instead of rounded shapes.

Pasteur's private laboratory notes have only been made public relatively recently. They reveal that he was driven at least as much by his own scientific interest, as by a desire to help the local community—although in the end, his work has been of huge benefit to people all around the world.

However, Pasteur may not have been as much of a sudden hero as this story indicates. From his own notes, it seems he had been interested in the process of fermentation for some time, not to help his community, but because some of the alcohols that were made did not seem to fit in with his theories on **crystal** shapes.

Fermentation

In 1857, Louis Pasteur decided to change the whole thrust of his research. He left behind his obsession with the details of **asymmetrical molecules** and **crystals,** and moved on to something with far wider appeal—**fermentation,** and why fermenting liquids are **optically active.** His work would have far-reaching effects on the brewing of beer and the production of wine, right up to the present day.

In the meantime, his wife Marie worked hard behind the scenes, acting as his secretary, listening to his ideas, and bringing up their children.

A new way of seeing

Fermentation had long been regarded as a process of disintegration—people thought that the sugar that was needed for the formation of alcoholic drinks broke down, and one of the products of this breakdown was **alcohol.** Pasteur knew this could not be right. Sugar is optically active, but once it is broken down, the activity ends. So where was the optical activity he measured in alcohols coming from? Pasteur knew that only living organisms are capable of creating new, asymmetrical molecules, so he reasoned that fermentation itself must be a living process.

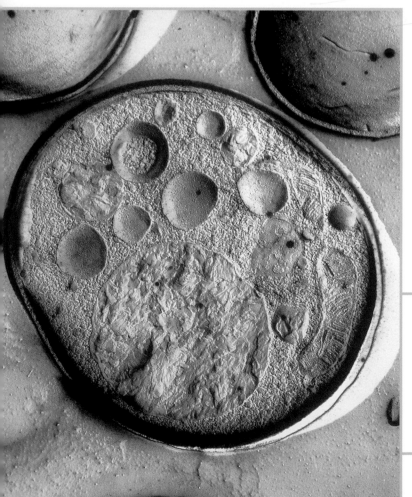

This yeast cell is magnified many times. Pasteur showed that fermentation is brought about by living yeast cells such as these—a breakthrough for the makers of beer and wine.

Fermentations on the scale that this massive brewery requires would simply not be possible if Louis Pasteur had not found out about the tiny microorganisms that make it happen, and the conditions they like to work in.

Pasteur showed that fermentation produces not just carbon dioxide and ethanol, but also other chemicals, such as succinic acid. He emphasized the complexity of fermentation and used this to confirm his ideas that the reactions must be linked to a living organism. He went on to prove this experimentally. If yeast is mixed with pure sugar solution and ammonium nitrate, then alcohol is formed. If any of the ingredients are removed, then no fermentation takes place.

ONGOING IMPACT   Wines and beers

When Louis Pasteur showed that fermentation is a process brought about by a living organism, it had enormous implications for the brewing industry and wine producers. Living organisms need carefully controlled conditions. They function best if their waste products are removed regularly, and the temperature at which they work is crucial. Pasteur's discovery has made it possible for brewing and wine-making to change from small-scale, local industries to large, factory-based operations, with millions of gallons fermented every week.

Spontaneous Generation

For centuries, people had believed in **spontaneous generation,** or the idea that living things come into being spontaneously by the will of God. But by Louis Pasteur's time, some people were beginning to doubt the idea. This doubt led to other problems, since it implied a lack of belief in the power of God. There was no clear evidence either way. Someone needed to conclude the debate—and this is what Pasteur set out to do.

Félix-Archimède Pouchet (1800–1872) was nearly 60, a respected naturalist from Rouen in northwest France, when he came into conflict with the 37-year-old Louis Pasteur over spontaneous generation. Pouchet had had a long career in traditional biology, specializing in the development of embryos and reproductive biology. He was director of the Natural History Museum in Rouen and a member of the **Académie des Sciences** in Paris.

Did frogs emerge from mud and molds spontaneously appear on food by the will of God, as people believed, or from cells and organisms that were already there? Louis Pasteur was determined to find out.

After a long and distinguished career, Pouchet had decided that under certain circumstances, living cells arose spontaneously and then developed into adult organisms. In 1858, he published a paper in which he claimed to prove that this type of spontaneous generation had occurred in an experiment he had carried out. He claimed that microorganisms had appeared in boiled hay infusions, which he had stored under mercury after exposing them to oxygen. In 1859, he then produced an enormous book on the theory of spontaneous generation, in which he brought together all the evidence he could find to support his theory. He included experimental evidence, evidence from embryo development, and theological and religious views, claiming they all showed he was right. Many dedicated supporters agreed with his findings.

Félix-Archimède Pouchet was a well-respected member of the scientific community and certainly no lightweight opponent for Pasteur!

Pasteur's initial response to Pouchet was very quiet, for he had done very little work on spontaneous generation. However, the work that he had done suggested that microorganisms only appeared in such a mixture if air was allowed to enter. Therefore, Pasteur thought that the microorganisms that appeared in Pouchet's broth had almost certainly already been present in air that had accidentally been admitted to the experiment. He wrote an almost apologetic letter to Pouchet suggesting that this might be the explanation—but within a year, this polite exchange of ideas had been replaced by a furious and rather bitter quarrel.

The Swan-necked Flasks

Louis Pasteur became determined to show that ordinary air contained living organisms, and that it did not possess some "mysterious principle" that caused **spontaneous generation** when conditions were right.

At the same time, he and Marie suffered the loss of their oldest child, Jeanne. She died of typhoid fever, one of many widespread **infectious diseases** at the time. The death of nine-year-old Jeanne hit Pasteur hard, but he still pressed on with his work.

The proof of the theory

Pasteur showed that if he pumped atmospheric air through a plug of cotton wool, it became full of microscopic living organisms. Pasteur believed it was these organisms that started to grow when air got into any sealed vessel. He went on to set up three elegant experiments to prove once and for all that spontaneous generation did not occur.

First, Pasteur cleverly tried Pouchet's own method, and found that even in his own expert hands, the method gave very inconsistent results. This finding encouraged him to continue.

Second, he boiled a sugar and yeast solution in a flask, killed the yeast so that nothing could grow, filled the flask with **sterile** air, and then sealed it in a hot flame. Nothing grew in it for six weeks—then Pasteur introduced one of his wads of cotton wool loaded with microbes from the air and sealed the flask again. Within 36 hours, the liquid in the flask was teeming with familiar microorganisms.

Pasteur believed—rightly—that microorganisms like these were the source of the life that developed in the sealed flasks.

Pasteur suggested that the growth in the fluid must come from the microbes in the air. He knew that some of his opponents would still be unconvinced—he could imagine them arguing that life had spontaneously generated from the organic material in the cotton wool—so he repeated the experiment using asbestos, a mineral material, and got exactly the same results.

The swan-necked flasks

Now, Pasteur felt he had proved that nothing was needed for microbial life beyond the germs found in the air itself. It was the beginning of his germ theory. He published his first findings in February 1860. By May, he had extended his work to growths on milk and urine. Pouchet's ideas were finished, and **pasteurization** was just around the corner.

In 1863, Marie gave birth to their fifth child, a baby daughter whom they named Camille.

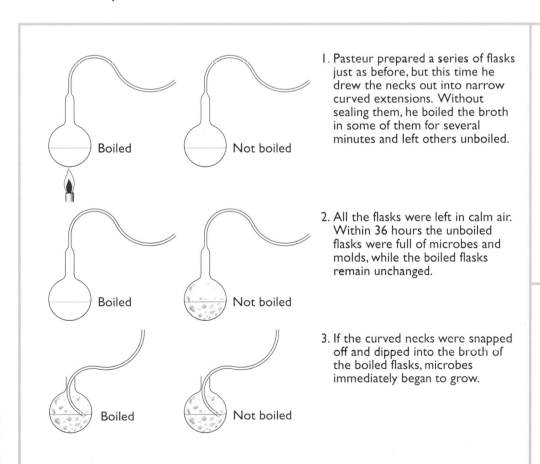

1. Pasteur prepared a series of flasks just as before, but this time he drew the necks out into narrow curved extensions. Without sealing them, he boiled the broth in some of them for several minutes and left others unboiled.

2. All the flasks were left in calm air. Within 36 hours the unboiled flasks were full of microbes and molds, while the boiled flasks remain unchanged.

3. If the curved necks were snapped off and dipped into the broth of the boiled flasks, microbes immediately began to grow.

From the elegant simplicity of these experiments, Louis Pasteur concluded that the "swan necks" trapped germs from the air, preventing them from reaching the broth and growing.

The Silkworm Crisis

In the eighteenth and nineteenth centuries, France had a flourishing silkworm industry worth ten million francs a year. No wonder the mulberry—the tree whose leaves the silkworm eats—was called "the tree of gold"! But by the early 1860s, a mysterious disease was destroying the silkworms, and the silk industry was falling apart.

The problem

The disease **pébrine** attacked silkworms at any stage of their life cycle. The main symptom was little black or brown spots appearing, followed rapidly by the death of the silkworm or moth. The disease first appeared in 1845, and by 1864, it was widespread in France, Italy, Spain, Austria—even China was attacked. Eventually, Japan was the only remaining disease-free country, and

The silkworm is not a worm at all—it is the caterpillar of the silk moth. It turned out to be vulnerable to the new and deadly disease pébrine in every stage of its life cycle.

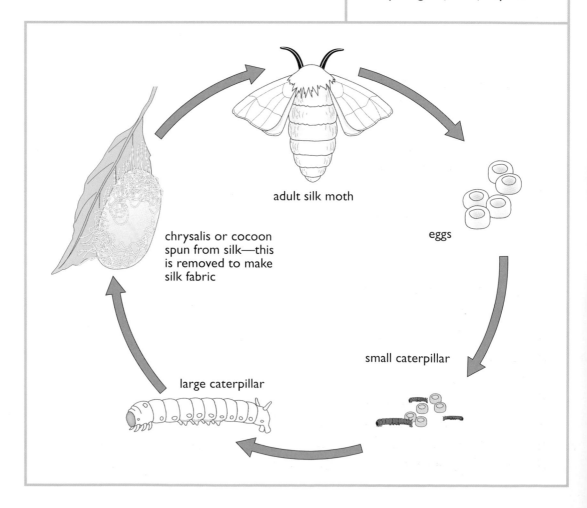

adult silk moth

eggs

chrysalis or cocoon spun from silk—this is removed to make silk fabric

small caterpillar

large caterpillar

healthy silkworm eggs had to be bought from there. The livelihood of thousands of people was being destroyed, and poverty, starvation, and disease followed close behind.

In desperation, J. B. Dumas, a French government official, wrote to Louis Pasteur, appealing to him to come to the aid of one of France's most important industries. Pasteur had solved the problems of the brewers and the wine-makers. Could he now save the silkworms?

The solution

In June 1865, Louis Pasteur arrived in Alais (now called Alès) to begin his research, having read everything he could about silkworms. He had to wait months for moths to develop before the results of each investigation were made fully clear. Yet within three years of traveling between Alais and his home in Paris, he had devised a way by which growers could be sure that their eggs—and therefore the caterpillars that would hatch out of them—were clear of disease.

Pasteur did all this immensely valuable work at a time of great personal sadness. In June 1865, his beloved father died, and in September, his youngest daughter, two-year-old Camille, died too. Camille's death came after weeks of fever. Louis and Marie had sat up night after night nursing their child, and her death left them both exhausted and brokenhearted.

In Pasteur's words:

Pasteur was very concerned at the request from Dumas, and not at all sure that he had the expertise to help. He wrote:

"Your proposition…is indeed most flattering and the object is a high one, but it troubles and embarrasses me! Remember, if you please, that I have never even touched a silkworm. If I had some of your knowledge of the subject I should not hesitate…"

In Pasteur's words:

To his great sorrow, Louis was not with his father when he died. He wrote a touching and affectionate letter to his wife and children from Alais to tell them what had happened.

"For thirty years I have been his constant care, I owe everything to him. When I was young he kept me from bad company and instilled into me the habit of working …How glad I am that he saw you all again a short time ago, and that he lived to know little Camille."

23

Louis Pasteur was always grateful to his parents for the support they gave him as he grew up, and for their ability to accept and encourage his desire for learning. His mother died when he was still a young man, but his father lived to realize that through Louis, the name of Pasteur would be remembered for a very long time.

The family man

Pasteur was not the most attentive husband—his work was too absorbing for that—but Marie accepted this, acting as his helpmate, partner, and secretary. On their 35th wedding anniversary, she wrote to their surviving daughter, Marie-Louise, "Your father, very busy as always, says little to me!" In spite of this, Louis's marriage to Marie was long and successful, lasting for 46 years.

Their son, Jean-Baptiste, never had any children, which disappointed Pasteur. He would have liked to see the family name continue. It then fell to his only surviving daughter, Marie-Louise, born in 1858, to produce the longed-for grandson. She married René Vallery-Radot, a popular writer who would later produce a masterly biography of his father-in-law, and they named their son Louis Pasteur Vallery-Radot.

Marie Pasteur supported her husband's work throughout their marriage and was described by one fellow scientist as "his greatest collaborator."

But this is leaping forward into the future. In the late 1860s, Pasteur was a well-established scientist, respected by many people, but known and liked by fewer. Some people were put off by his stern manner and dedication to work, yet he was loyal and supportive of those he thought were worthy of his friendship. He was tremendously organized and fastidiously clean. His understanding of the role of invisible microorganisms in causing disease may have been behind his frequent washing—not only of his hands, but of his eating and drinking utensils as well!

Struck down in his prime

On October 19, 1868, when Louis Pasteur was 45 years old and achieving great things, disaster struck. He suffered a severe stroke that left him paralyzed down his left side and badly affected his speech. He was given the best treatment that was available, including bleeding with sixteen leeches, and was nursed devotedly by Marie. As a result, he recovered sufficiently to take up his life and work once again, but his speech, walking, and ability to use his hands were affected for the rest of his life. His great mind was unaffected, but in the future, the ideas and experiments Pasteur dreamed up would have to be carried out mainly by the hands of others.

Louis and Marie had five children, whom they adored. Louis was rather active in their care for a man of his generation, and it was a cause of great distress to him that Jeanne, Camille, and finally Cécile died as children. This picture shows Louis and Marie in 1892 with their only son, Jean-Baptiste, their sole surviving daughter, Marie-Louise, her husband, and their grandchildren.

Fighting Infectious Diseases

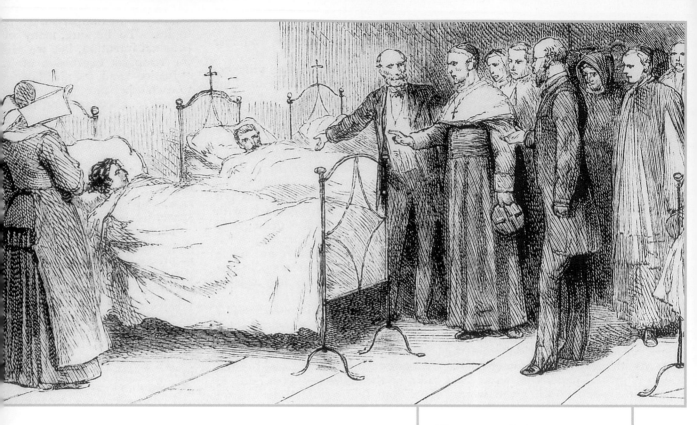

When Louis Pasteur announced his intention to move the focus of his research to the study of **infectious diseases,** the delighted French government granted him the money to build and equip a new laboratory to use for this very purpose.

This was a cholera ward in a nineteenth-century hospital. Thousands of men, women, and children died of infectious diseases at this time. Three of Pasteur's own little daughters were among them.

Building in Paris had started just before Pasteur suffered his stroke, and since he was expected to die, the work ground to a halt. Pasteur could see and hear the building site from his home, and as he began to recover, he found the lack of progress on his new laboratory deeply distressing. When Emperor Napoleon III heard of this, he wrote personally to ensure that building work started again immediately. Greatly enthused, Pasteur prepared to return to work—against his doctors' advice—only three months after his stroke. The great new laboratory was completed in 1871, but Pasteur did not actually begin his work on infectious diseases until 1877.

The curse of infection

It is hard for us, at the start of a new millennium, to realize how terrible the scourge of infection was in the nineteenth century. There were no **antibiotics** to stop infections. Surgery was very dangerous, because the almost inevitable infection of the wound meant that operations usually resulted in death. In maternity hospitals, almost a quarter of women died from infection in the first few days after giving birth. It was this helplessness and suffering that made Pasteur determined to find out the cause of these infections and prevent them.

JOSEPH LISTER

Joseph Lister (1827–1912) was a British surgeon who read Pasteur's germ theory of **fermentation** and made the mental leap that it might be similar "germs" that cause infection. He developed the use of **carbolic acid** to kill those germs and prevent infection during and after surgery. In Lister's wards, all of the surgical instruments and dressings were sterilized in carbolic solution before use. The surgeons and their assistants washed their hands in carbolic solution before operating or changing dressings. In the operating room, a fine spray of carbolic acid was used to create an **antiseptic** atmosphere. In 1874, Lister wrote to Pasteur, telling him of his progress and expressing gratitude for the way in which Pasteur's work had helped him in his thinking.

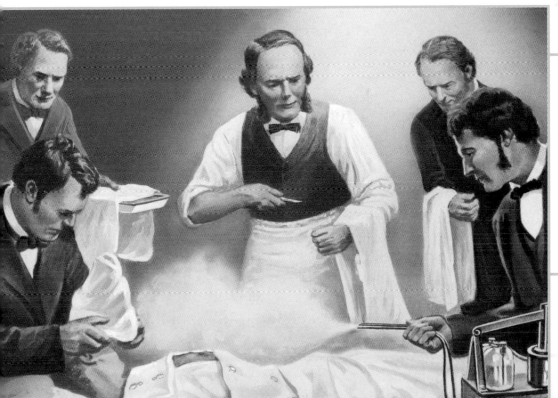

Lister introduced the revolutionary idea of sterile operating rooms and hospitals, and the survival rates of patients soared.

The Battle Against Anthrax

Anthrax is caused by the bacterium *Bacillus anthracis*. The blood of the affected animal becomes packed with bacteria; large, swollen, blistering pustules form on the body; and **septicemia** sets in. It is almost always fatal and can attack humans as well as farm animals, entering through broken skin. Most frighteningly, anthrax **spores** survive in the soil for many years.

The search for a vaccine

Between 10 and 50 percent of French flocks of sheep and herds of cattle were being lost to charbon or splenic fever—as anthrax was known—each year. Pasteur and his team were confident of producing a **vaccine** for anthrax, but it was not as easy as they hoped. The bacterium proved difficult to grow at first, and then seemed impossible to make safe.

Pasteur tried all sorts of treatments—heat, chemicals such as potassium bichromate, and oxygen—yet none seemed to give reliable results. To add to the pressure, Jean-Joseph Henri Toussaint, a young veterinarian, claimed to have produced a

The Scottish island of Gruinard, in the distance, was infected with anthrax spores during World War II as part of an exercise in germ warfare. It remained uninhabitable for over 40 years.

successful vaccine by heating blood infected with anthrax to 131°F (55°C) for ten minutes. Pasteur discovered that a vaccine produced in this way was very unreliable, and in February 1881 he announced that he too had developed a new anthrax vaccine. Because he was such a well-known figure, people paid more attention to Pasteur's vaccine.

Scientific development on Pasteur's vaccine was then interrupted by a very public challenge to demonstrate its effectiveness. This was issued by Hippolyte Rossignol, a veterinary surgeon who had little or no time for Pasteur's germ theory. Rather than look unsure of his science, Pasteur accepted the challenge, though he was not certain that his vaccine would work!

The trial at Pouilly-le-Fort

1. On May 5, 25 sheep were given Pasteur's anthrax vaccine. Another group of 25 similar sheep was given no vaccine. This was repeated on May 17, using a stronger dose of the vaccine.
2. On May 31, all 50 sheep were injected with active anthrax spores. Pasteur predicted that the vaccinated sheep would survive.
3. On June 2, scientists, the press, and the public gathered at Pouilly-le-Fort to see the results. The vaccinated sheep were all alive. The unvaccinated sheep were mostly dead, and the rest were dying of anthrax.

After the triumph at Pouilly-le-Fort, Pasteur completed the development of his vaccine, which had a major effect on farming for generations to come. At home, too, he was enjoying the fruits of family life. His son, Jean-Baptiste, was married and had become a diplomat, and his daughter, Marie-Louise, had married the writer René Vallery-Radot.

Rabies

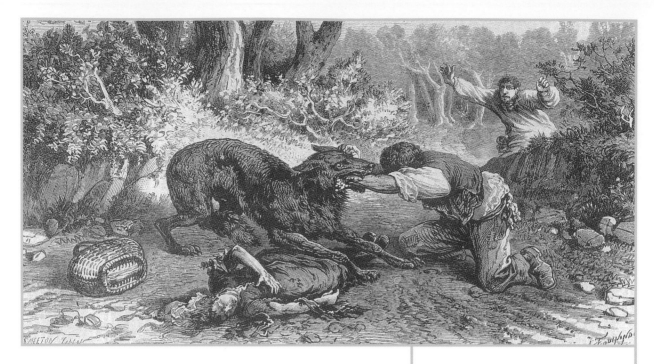

In Louis Pasteur's time, rabies was very rare in people, as it is today. Yet rabies struck fear into the bravest heart. The **incubation period** could be months or even years after the bite of a rabid animal, and once the symptoms started to show, there was no hope—death was certain.

Rabies is also known as hydrophobia, meaning "fear of water." Eventually, sufferers cannot even bear to swallow their own saliva. This picture from a nineteenth-century French magazine shows a rabid dog attacking a group of people.

The horror of the disease is made clear in the 1794 account of the death of an English weaver on the facing page. Even today, the course of rabies is still dreadful without **vaccination.** There are pools of infection in wild animals in many parts of the world, including much of Europe and the United States.

Pasteur's choice

As a boy, Louis Pasteur had been deeply affected by the attack of a rabid wolf on his own village, and now as an eminent scientist, he decided he must turn his attention to rabies. There were not even 50 human cases of rabies in France in most years, but rabid animals were relatively common, and the disease so dramatic, that Pasteur could not resist attempting to find a **vaccine.** He knew that if he was successful, not only would great fame and glory be his, but it would also prove his germ theory once and for all to those who were still skeptical.

The rabies microbe

Pasteur wanted desperately to find the microbe that was causing rabies, and he searched for it in the saliva, blood, and brains of infected animals. He never found it, but he was still sure that a microbe was causing the disease, and that he would be able to *culture,* or grow, it, weaken its intensity, and produce a vaccine.

In May 1794, a weaver named John Lindsay arrived at a hospital in Manchester, England. He was terrified that he might have rabies, as a result of a rabid dog bite many years previously. When asked to drink a little cold water, he could hardly get any down, and he was frightened by any noise or person approaching. Over the next couple of days, doctors were distressed to see the way he struggled to swallow food or liquid.

John was frantic to prove he did not have rabies because he had a wife and six young children to support. Despite his determination, however, the disease took hold. He began to twitch and spasm at the slightest sound or touch. He had difficulty breathing and severe pain in his stomach and chest. He could not swallow his saliva, and began to spit constantly. John had terrifying hallucinations, yet he could still answer questions quite sensibly. A short time later, his racing heart began to falter. Finally, the poor man had a massive convulsion and died.

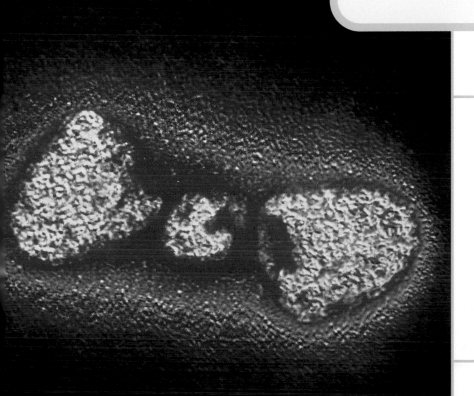

The rabies virus is so small that it would have passed through every filter and been invisible to even the most powerful microscope available when Pasteur was working. Today, the modern technology of the electron microscope allows us to see it.

Young Joseph Meister was bitten by a rabid dog more than a dozen times on his hands, thighs, and calves. The bites were so deep he could hardly walk, yet Pasteur's experimental vaccine saved his life.

Pasteur studied rabies off and on for several years, but time and time again, he returned to his research. With Pasteur hot on the trail, it was only a matter of time before the problem of rabies was solved.

One of the biggest problems facing research into rabies was that in dogs, symptoms only developed a month or more after infection. Pierre-Victor Galtier, a veterinary surgeon in Lyon, discovered that rabies could be transmitted to rabbits, shortening the **incubation period** to eighteen days. Galtier also had other ideas that Pasteur picked up and secretly worked on, until in 1884, he went public with some amazing news—he had discovered a way of producing weakened **vaccines** that could make dogs **immune** to rabies itself.

Then all went quiet again until …

Human "guinea pigs"

On Monday, July 6, 1885, three terrified visitors arrived at Louis Pasteur's laboratory. Two of them had been bitten by a rabid dog two days earlier. The dog's owner was safe, since his skin had not been punctured, but little Joseph Meister, comforted by his frantic mother, was not as lucky. Two separate doctors agreed that the child faced certain death from rabies. So, with the family's permission, Pasteur set out to treat him with a technique that had so far been tried only on dogs.

Over eleven days, Joseph was given thirteen injections of the rabies virus, each a little stronger than the last. After that, the boy went home— and never developed rabies. Pasteur was jubilant, but told no one except his wife Marie and their two remaining children, who remained closely in touch with their father and his work even though they had married and moved away.

Three months later, Pasteur heard about a fifteen-year-old shepherd, Jean-Baptiste Jupille. When he and other shepherds had been attacked by a rabid dog, Jean-Baptiste saved the younger boys by fighting and killing the vicious dog—but he was severely bitten himself. Was there anything Pasteur could do to help save this brave and selfless young man?

Pasteur was Jean-Baptiste's only chance—and the vaccine worked. The grueling series of injections gave him immunity from the disease, and he returned home cured. The prevention of rabies was the final major discovery of Pasteur's long and distinguished career, and it ensured his place in the history books.

Pasteur immediately agreed to treat local hero Jean-Baptiste Jupille, but warned that the chances of success were lower than when Joseph Meister was treated because the treatment would be starting several days after the bite. To his delight, the young man survived.

The Man and the Myth

Louis Pasteur was a great man and a great scientist—of that there is no doubt. But there are two sides to everyone, and as Pasteur's private notebooks have become public, people have learned more about his doubts and hesitations. While most scientists welcomed a free exchange of ideas, he was a very secretive worker. He would work for a long time before publishing any results—partly, it seems, to prevent fellow scientists from using his work.

The Pastorians

This secrecy was made possible by the dedication of Pasteur's wife, Marie, who throughout their marriage acted as his confidante, and by the group of loyal workers Pasteur built up around himself, who became known as the Pastorians. This group, which included Dr. Émile Roux, worked to support Pasteur and to carry out the tasks he could not manage himself. They left it to the "Master" to decide when the results should be made public.

On the other hand, Pasteur himself was always ready to use the ideas of other scientists to help him overcome a particular problem. While in some cases he acknowledged the help he received, there were times when he simply used other people's results without giving them any credit.

Researchers who worked with Pasteur were expected to show fierce loyalty to both the man and his ideas. Whenever questions about Pasteur's ethics or methods were raised, his supporters could simply answer: look at his results!

Here, Pasteur works in his laboratory in 1885. In his private laboratory notebooks, he confided many misgivings and concerns.

Hidden doubts

Pasteur's public image was of a supremely confident man who never allowed any uncertainty to show. Everyone knew about his successes in treating the boys bitten by rabid dogs. However, the release of his private laboratory notebooks in 1971 showed that Pasteur had earlier treated two other people bitten by rabid dogs.

In 1885, he treated a 61-year-old man who probably never had rabies, and an 11-year-old girl named Julie-Antoinette Poughon, who had been bitten on the lip by her own puppy, which had become rabid. She received two injections of Pasteur's **vaccine** but died of rabies within a day. These two were never mentioned publicly by Pasteur. Only two weeks after the death of little Julie-Antoinette, he tried out a new method—this time successfully—on Joseph Meister.

A strong man

Unlike many scientists, Louis Pasteur was very politically aware. He knew who to influence and how to ensure that he and his family were well provided for financially. Louis would discuss his work passionately with his wife and children, revealing his insecurities and concerns, but he never allowed any such "weaknesses" to be made public. After suffering a debilitating stroke while still in his prime, he drove himself on to make some of the most influential scientific and medical discoveries of the nineteenth century.

This flask of Pasteur's contains the dried spinal cord of a rabbit that had died of rabies. Pasteur was convinced that his new method of preparing a rabies vaccine using dried spinal cords would prove effective, even though it wasn't properly tested before he tried it.

Journey's End

The French government, recognizing the immense implications of Pasteur's work on germ theory and **vaccination,** invested heavily in a superb research complex in which he could carry on his work. This great building was to be known as l'Institut Pasteur (the Pasteur Institute). It was completed in 1888, but after suffering a further series of small strokes in 1887, Pasteur was never well enough to work in his own laboratories.

In his old age, Pasteur took great comfort from his only grandson.

The overseer

Pasteur's failing health did not cloud his mind, however. Although he could no longer work actively himself, he could oversee and supervise the group of other researchers and students—the Pastorians—who were following in his footsteps. They took it upon themselves to carry on the work of the "Master" and began to tackle yet another of the dreaded **infectious diseases** of the time. **Diphtheria** killed thousands of children every year, and the workers at the Pasteur Institute prepared to produce a **vaccine** against it.

By this stage, Pasteur was becoming increasingly frail. He was receiving honors from all over the world as countries across the globe benefited from the work he had done. There was no **Nobel prize** for science or medicine in Pasteur's day—but if there had been, he would surely have received it at least once, if not twice. When he turned 70, he was presented with a medal inscribed: "To Pasteur, on his seventieth birthday. France and Humanity grateful"—summing up the worldwide recognition of his work.

Death

The infirmities of age began to close in on Louis Pasteur. In 1894, he suffered another stroke, and by his death, he was almost completely paralyzed. When his final illness set in, he was nursed night and day by a combination of his family and his work colleagues. Marie, his devoted wife, spent most of her time at his bedside, and his beloved grandchildren came in each day to cuddle him and talk. In spite of all their care, Louis Pasteur died in the afternoon of Saturday, September 28, 1895, at the age of 72.

A nation mourns

The death of Louis Pasteur affected the whole French nation, for he had brought great honor and fame to his country and had benefited the whole human race.

After a period of lying in state in the Pasteur Institute, Pasteur was given a grand state funeral on October 5, 1895, after which his body was returned to an ornate mausoleum in the institute that bore his name. The whole country mourned the death of a man who, in his life's work, had saved the lives of so many others in France and around the world.

After his death, the body of Louis Pasteur lay in state in an ornate room in the Pasteur Institute.

Pasteur's Legacy

Louis Pasteur lived and worked in the nineteenth century, a time when many modern ideas about science and medicine were only just beginning to emerge. In one way or another, his legacy touches us all.

In the euphoria that surrounded Pasteur's later work, it is easy to forget his early success in the field of **tartrates** and **isomers.** His discovery of isomers that rotate **polarized light** in different directions has had far-reaching implications both in materials science—the science of matter—and in biochemistry. There is now a branch of science known as **stereochemistry,** which studies the arrangement of **atoms** and **molecules** in space. The **optical activity** of substances is an important aspect of this discipline, and it all began with Louis Pasteur and his dedicated work.

Pasteurized milk has had an enormous impact on the health of people in many countries, especially by reducing the spread of diseases like tuberculosis.

Good wine, good beer, safe milk

Across the world, the brewing industry and wine producers have an enormous impact both on people's social lives and on the economies of nations. By unfolding the secrets of the processes that make wine and beer sour, Pasteur made possible the enormous expansion of these industries, which could now produce large quantities of reliable products. Milk that is safe to drink is another of Pasteur's important legacies. **Pasteurizing** milk kills off most of the harmful bacteria it contains, which means we can drink it without the risk of catching diseases like tuberculosis (TB). The milk also lasts longer before going bad.

TB is a disease caused by bacteria that attack the lungs in particular. It was a major killer in Pasteur's time, and is still a relatively common cause of death in many countries.

The battle against disease

It is in the battle against the devastation of **infectious disease** that the work of Louis Pasteur has had its greatest effect. It was largely due to Pasteur that scientists, doctors, and the public accepted the idea that diseases are spread by germs, or microbes. This key realization alone, which seems so obvious now, has saved millions of lives. People now understand the importance of hygiene in everyday life, and the risk of infection between a sick and a healthy individual.

However, it was perhaps Pasteur's work on **vaccination** that has had the most dramatic legacy. Many of the most virulent and dangerous infectious diseases in people and domestic animals are now controlled by vaccination, and others may be soon.

While experimenting in the 1860s, Pasteur realized that the microbes that caused milk to go bad, and **fermentations** to fail, could be killed by heat, and that liquids treated in this way would last for much longer. It soon became common practice to treat milk, beer, and other liquids with heat to preserve them. The process was known as "pasteurization" in honor of Pasteur.

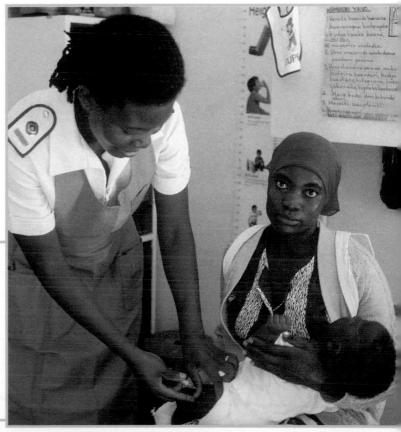

A baby in Zimbabwe receives a vaccination. The life expectancy of young children in the developed world, and increasingly in the developing world, has been greatly increased by vaccinations against the most common childhood diseases.

L'Institut Pasteur

Another crucial aspect of the legacy of Louis Pasteur is the institute of scientific research which bears his name. Founded by Pasteur and inaugurated in 1888, l'Institut Pasteur is a private, nonprofit organization. It was originally set up in Paris as a center for the treatment of rabies, a research center for **infectious diseases,** and a teaching center. It is still all of these things.

Pasteur was committed not only to basic research, but also to its practical applications. Those who have followed after him have maintained this tradition, from Émile Roux and Alexandre Yersin, who both worked with Pasteur himself, to the scientists working with the Institute today.

Some great scientists...

Many famous scientists have worked at the Pasteur Institute. Roux and Yersin discovered a treatment for **diphtheria,** a major killer—particularly of children. Many **Nobel prize** winners have also emerged from the Institute:

- Elie Metchnikoff, in 1908, for contributions to the understanding of the **immune** system, which fights disease in the body
- Jules Bordet, in 1919, for discoveries about immunity to diseases
- Charles Nicolle, in 1928, for his work on the way typhus— a disease that had been a complete mystery for many years— is transmitted
- François Jacob, Jacques Monod, and André Lwoff, in 1965, for shedding light on how viruses are regulated in body cells.

More than a century after the death of Louis Pasteur, scientific research goes on, both at the original Pasteur Institute in Paris shown here, and at other branches of the Institute set up in countries around the world.

...and great science

Much of modern preventative medicine has its origins in the Pasteur Institute. **Vaccinations** against diphtheria, tetanus, tuberculosis, yellow fever, polio, and **hepatitis B** were all developed there, along with the use of antibacterial drugs for treating bacterial infections. Since World War II, the Institute has focused on **molecular** biology. In recent years, scientists at the Institute have discovered HIV, the virus responsible for **AIDS,** as well as the bacterium responsible for causing many stomach ulcers. They have produced a **genetically engineered vaccine** against hepatitis B and developed tests for the early detection of colon cancer and *Helicobacter pylori.*

This blood cell is infected with HIV, the virus that causes the dreadful disease AIDS. Its discovery in the 1980s was one of the Pasteur Institute's greatest triumphs.

The Pasteur Institute in Paris now houses 100 research units, with hundreds of scientists from 70 countries working there. It runs a teaching hospital, and is at the center of a global network of over two dozen Pasteur Institutes. It is a fitting memorial to a remarkable man.

A Giant among Giants

The work of Louis Pasteur has had an enormous impact on human lives and the way in which society has developed since he first made his remarkable discoveries.

When Pasteur began his scientific work as a young man, a lot of the accepted explanations for disease had not been challenged for many, many years. Most people believed that life was spontaneously created by God wherever molds or other organisms seemed to appear suddenly without any other known cause. By the time Pasteur died, though, much of the old belief had been proven wrong, and a more modern, scientific view of the world was accepted by experts and the public alike.

The list of his achievements is long—**stereochemistry,** beer and wine production, **pasteurization,** germ theory, **vaccination,** the defeat of rabies—and it continues to grow through the research done in his name at the Pasteur Institutes throughout the world.

F^r. BOURNAND

ancien éléve de l'École des hautes Études.

Un bienfaiteur de l'Humanité.

PASTEUR.

sa vie, son œuvre.

Quand on a bien étudié, on revient à la foi du paysan breton. Si j'avais étudié plus encore, j'aurais la foi de la paysanne bretonne.

PASTEUR.

TOLRA & M. SIMONET   ÉDITEURS Succ^rs
28, Rue d'Assas, 28, PARIS   MAITREJEAN inv. s. del 18.

This tribute to Pasteur is entitled: "A Benefactor of Humanity." Not many scientists receive this type of honor when they die!

42

Current research includes the study of cancer and the search for **vaccines** against many diseases, including **AIDS** and tropical diseases such as **malaria, dengue,** and those caused by the *Shigella* bacterium. The expertise of the Pastorians in just this type of work leads to hope that they will soon find some answers.

A scientist of genius

Louis Pasteur was a man whose scientific work was of such immense value to his fellow people that he achieved greatness and appreciation during his own lifetime, not just among the scientific community, but also among ordinary people. They might not have understood exactly what Pasteur was doing, but they certainly recognized that they and their children were more likely to live because of it.

That sense of greatness has not diminished with time. We still recognize that in Louis Pasteur we were visited by one of the truly great scientists. His influence will continue on into the future, because his discoveries and his visions were ones that will not fade.

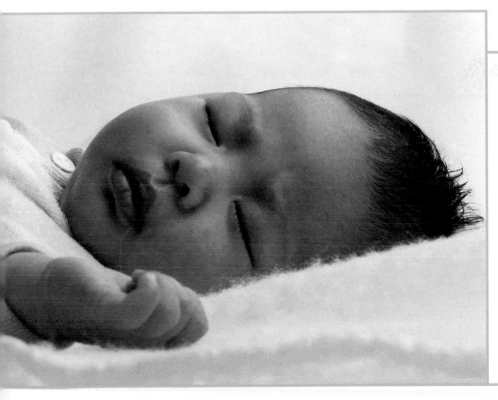

Babies and their parents can sleep more peacefully with the knowledge that through the work of Louis Pasteur—on hygiene in hospital wards, on pasteurizing milk, and on vaccination against serious diseases—a baby born in today's world stands a good chance of growing into a healthy adult.

Timeline

1789	The **French Revolution** begins.
1815	Napoleon is defeated.
1816	Louis's parents, Jean-Joseph Pasteur and Jeanne Etiennette Roqui, are married.
1822	Louis Pasteur is born on December 27, in Dôle, in eastern France.
1831	In October, a rabid wolf attacks people in Louis's home village of Arbois; eight people later die of rabies.
1831–39	Louis is a student at the Collège d'Arbois.
1839–42	Student at the Collège Royal in Besançon, where he earns his **baccalauréat;** also supervises other students.
1842–43	Student at the Pension Barbet and Lycée St. Louis, Paris.
1843–46	Studies at the École Normale, Paris; he also teaches there.
1847	Becomes a doctor of science and begins to study **crystals** and the **optical activity** of **tartrates.**
1848	Paris is rocked by revolution, and the Second Republic is declared.
	Jeanne Pasteur, Louis' mother, dies.
1849	Pasteur moves to Strasbourg University as professor of chemistry; on May 29, he marries Marie Laurent.
1850	Louis and Marie's first child is born, a daughter named Jeanne; they go on to have three more girls and a boy, but three of the children die in childhood.
1854–57	Pasteur is professor of chemistry and dean of the **Faculty** of Sciences at the University of Lille.
1863	Marie gives birth to their fifth child, a daughter named Camille.
1864	Pasteur introduces the process of **pasteurization.**
1865	Pasteur's father, Jean-Joseph, and his youngest daughter, Camille, both die.
	Joseph Lister extends Pasteur's work by developing the theory that germs cause infection, and introduces the use of **carbolic acid** as an **antiseptic** in operating rooms.
1865–69	Pasteur studies the silkworm disease **pébrine.**
1867–88	Director of the laboratory of physiological chemistry at the École Normale.
1868	Pasteur suffers a severe stroke that leaves him paralyzed down his left side. Despite this, he continues to work, with the help of his assistants, the "Pastorians."

1871	The French government builds a new laboratory for Pasteur in Paris, in which he later studies **infectious diseases.**
1877	Pasteur begins to study the causes and prevention of infectious diseases, including anthrax and rabies, in his new laboratory.
1885	Pasteur successfully treats two boys who have been infected with rabies.
1888	The Pasteur Institute, which Louis founded, is officially inaugurated in Paris as a center for the study of rabies and other infectious diseases.
1888–95	Pasteur is director of the Pasteur Institute, Paris.
1895	On September 28, Louis Pasteur dies at the age of 72.

More Books to Read

Birch, Beverley. *Pasteur's Fight against Microbes*. Hauppage, N.J.: Barron's Educational Series, Inc., 1995.

Newfield, Marcia. *The Life of Louis Pasteur*. Brookfield, Conn.: Twenty-First Century Books, Inc., 1995.

Smith, Linda W. *Louis Pasteur: Disease Fighter*. Berkeley Heights, N.J.: Enslow Publishers, Inc., 1997.

Glossary

Académie des Sciences organization of French scientists

AIDS Acquired Immune Deficiency Syndrome—disease that causes the breakdown of the human immune system and leaves the body open to attack by infectious diseases

alcohol common name for the chemical ethanol, C_2H_5OH, present in alcoholic drinks

antibiotic capable of destroying bacteria and curing diseases

antiseptic chemical that kills bacteria in the environment

aqueous humor liquid found in the front part of the eyeball

asymmetrical having sides that do not match

atom smallest particle of an element that has all its properties

baccalauréat French certificate of school completion

carbolic acid early antiseptic used by Lister

crystal solid in which the atoms are arranged in a regular pattern; crystals of the same substance always have the same basic shape

dengue type of tropical fever caused by a virus and spread by mosquitoes

diphtheria bacterial disease that affects the throat

faculty department or group of departments in a university

fermentation process by which sugar is broken down into ethanol and carbon dioxide by the action of yeast in low levels of oxygen

French Revolution (1789–1799) very violent time in France when people fought for reforms and the monarchy ended

genetically engineered made by artificially altering DNA, or genes

guillotine device for cutting people's heads off, widely used in the French Revolution

hepatitis B serious disease of the liver

immune protected or safe from a disease

incubation period time between exposure to an infectious agent and the appearance of the symptoms of disease

infectious disease disease caused by an infectious agent, such as a bacterium or a virus, that can be passed from one person to another

isomer substance composed of the same elements in the same proportions as another, but with different properties because of differences in the arrangements of the atoms

leather tanner person who preserves or cures animal skins to make them into flexible leather

malaria tropical disease of the blood spread by mosquitoes

militia group of armed people working for a particular leader or cause

molecule very small unit of a particular substance, usually made up of more than one atom joined together

Nobel prize annual prize for achievement in physics, chemistry, medicine, literature, economics, and work for peace

optically active having an effect on polarized light

pasteurization method of reducing the number of microorganisms present in liquids such as milk by heating, but not boiling

pébrine means "pepper"—silkworm disease that ravaged France and other silk-producing countries, characterized by tiny brown or black spots that appear on the animals

polarized light light in which the rays all travel in one direction

rector head of a university or school

septicemia blood poisoning caused by bacteria

Shigella type of bacterium that causes dysentery, a bowel infection

spontaneous generation appearance of living organisms from nothing, as a result of divine influence

spore "seed" of a fungus or bacterium

stereochemistry study of the arrangement of atoms and molecules in space

sterile free from microorganisms

tartrate salt of tartaric acid, which is found in plants and fruit

tenant farmer farmer who works land owned by someone else and pays rent in cash or by a share of the crop

vaccination method of inoculating someone with a strain of an infectious disease to prepare the immune system to fight, and thus prevent, the disease

vaccine weakened or dead strain of an infectious disease

Index